Buzzart Dikes, Kinloch, Perth and Kinross District: the
spectacular scenery of a medieval hunting park

IMAGES *of* SCOTLAND

EDINBURGH : HMSO

Top Argyll: stone-built chamber of a burial cairn *c.*3000BC

Bottom Argyll: standing stone with neolithic cup markings
*c.*2500BC

Opposite Fife: impressive setting of standing stones *c.*2500BC

Top Whitcastle Hill, Roxburgh District: fortifications and later
prehistoric farmsteads *c.*100BC

Bottom Green Castle, East Lothian: earthwork defences of
a medieval timber-built stronghold

Top Broch, near Bragar, Lewis

Bottom Spittal of Glenshee, Perth and Kinross District: medieval
cultivation strips around a long-abandoned farming settlement

Opposite Crannog, Loch Awe, Argyll: man-made island,
originally supporting timber houses, of a type common in the
Highlands *c.*800BC-AD1000

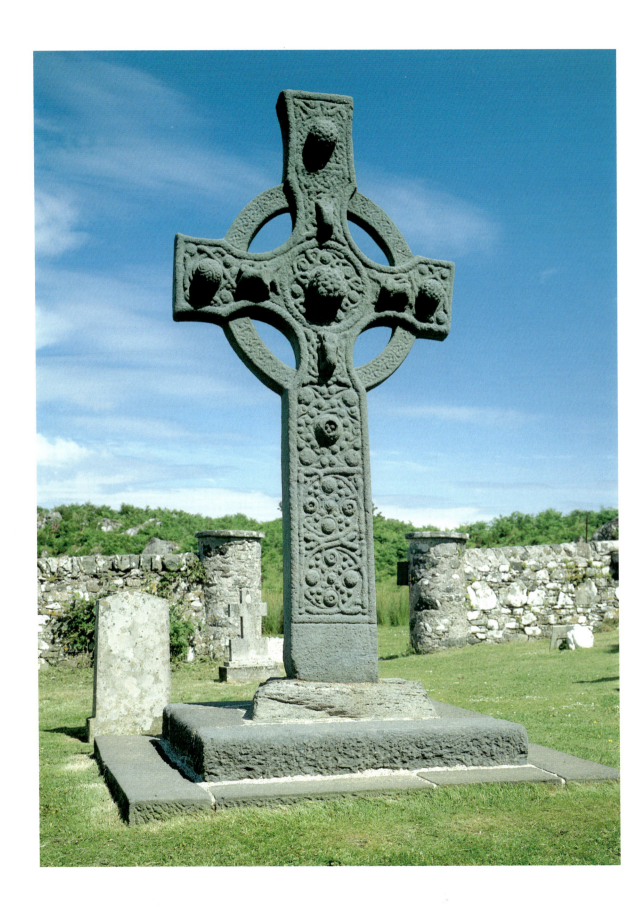

Left Pictish cross-slab, Meigle, Perth and Kinross District: rear
face showing a group of characteristic symbols *(Historic Scotland)*

Right Pictish cross-slab, Fowlis Wester, Perth and Kinross
District: the richly detailed carving includes Jonah's digestion
by the whale *(Historic Scotland)*

Opposite Kildalton Cross, Islay, Argyll *(Historic Scotland)*

Top Thatched cottage, Bousd, Isle of Coll, Argyll

Bottom Tobermory, Mull, Argyll: harbour and waterfront of
the planned village

Inveraray Castle and Town: view down Loch Fyne from
Dùn na Cuaiche

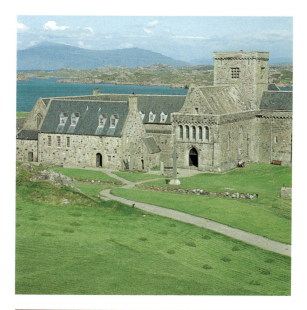

Top Iona Abbey and crosses, Argyll: general view
(Crosses, Historic Scotland)

Bottom Iona Abbey, Argyll: detail of restored cloister-arcade

Opposite Coats Memorial Church, Paisley, Renfrew District:
celestial vault over east end of mill owners' church

Top Medieval drain, Paisley Abbey, Renfrew District:
rib-vaulted cavern beneath the monastic precinct

Bottom Medieval drain, Paisley Abbey, Renfrew District:
round-arched bridge over eastern section

Opposite Leuchars Parish Church, North-East Fife: Romanesque
arcading on the south wall

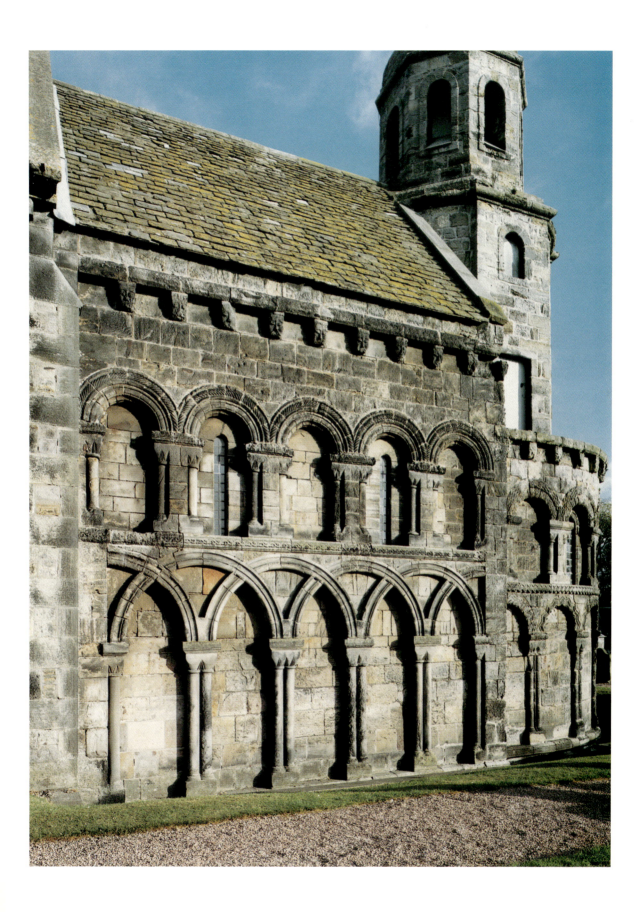

Top Caerlaverock Castle, Nithsdale: shield-shaped guardian of
the Solway frontier *(Historic Scotland)*

Bottom Fort George, Ardersier, Inverness District: the ultimate
in Hanoverian artillery fortification *(Historic Scotland)*

Opposite Dunderave Castle, Argyll: distant view of tower across
Loch Fyne towards Glen Kinglas

Top Glamis Castle, Angus: turreted entrance-front of
Strathmore's noble pile

Bottom Kinnaird Castle, Perth and Kinross District: life in a late
medieval tower, 20th-century style

Top Falkland Palace, North-East Fife: French Renaissance on
Scottish soil, courtyard façade of south quarter
(The National Trust for Scotland)

Bottom Kilchurn Castle, Loch Awe, Argyll: one-time fastness of
the Glenorchy Campbells *(Historic Scotland)*

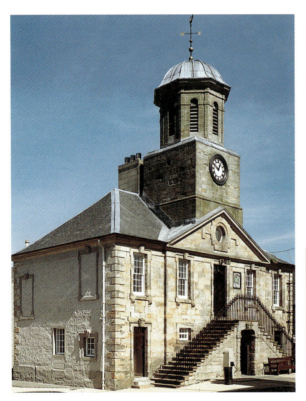 

Left Sanquhar Tolbooth (Town House), Nithsdale: Georgian
municipal building of William Adam design

Right Falkland Town House, North-East Fife: civic dignity
*c.*1800

Opposite Culross Town House, Dunfermline District
(*The National Trust for Scotland*)

22 Park Circus, Glasgow: cast-iron cupola, the crowning glory
of a rich mid-Victorian interior

Top Egyptian Halls, 84-100 Union Street, Glasgow: detail of
third-floor colonnade and 'Greek' Thomson ornament

Bottom India Tyre Factory, Inchinnan, Renfrew District: main
doorway to office-block

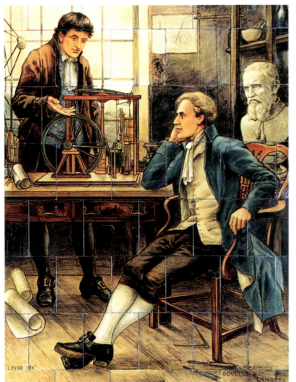

Café Royal, West Register Street, Edinburgh, sumptuous
turn-of-the-century interior: specimen tile pictures and stained-
glass window in Circle and Oyster Bars (James Watt; sailing
scene; and window representing archery and shooting)

Top Charcoal-fired iron furnace, Bonawe, Argyll *(Historic Scotland)*

Bottom Lady Victoria Colliery, Newtongrange, Midlothian,
in its National Coal Board heyday

Opposite Still-house, Tamdhu Distillery, Knockando, Moray:
bank of copper stills and early spirit-safe

Top Ornamental drinking-fountain, Maconochie Road,
Fraserburgh, Banff and Buchan

Bottom Kibble Palace, Botanic Gardens, Glasgow: a triumph of
glass and iron in the conservatory named after its designer

Opposite Glasgow School of Art, 167 Renfrew Street, Glasgow:
Charles Rennie Mackintosh insignia, window and bracket detail
on the north façade

Top Old bridge, Carrbridge, Badenoch and Strathspey District

Bottom Garron Bridge, Inveraray, Argyll

Opposite Forth Railway Bridge: track-level view through
latticed girders

Inclusion of sites within this booklet does not imply a right of public
access. Properties in the custody of the Secretary of State for Scotland
(Historic Scotland) and The National Trust for Scotland are indicated;
most of the remainder are in private ownership.

Copies of the views reproduced in this booklet may be purchased
on application to The Secretary, RCAHMS, John Sinclair House,
16 Bernard Terrace, Edinburgh EH8 9NX, citing the following
reference numbers:

John Knox's House B 47850 CT   Paisley, tile armorial B 44779 CN   Crathes A 27226 CN   Chamber of Burial Cairn: Argyll A 62844 CN
Standing Stone: Argyll A 62927 CT   Fife: standing stones B 77502 CT   Buzzart Dikes A 55549 CN   Whitcastle Hill B 17345 CN   Green Castle
A 56414 CN   Broch B 77503 CN   Spittal of Glenshee A 78041 CT   Crannog AG 4907 CN   Fowlis Wester A 35069 CN   Meigle B 1472 CN
Kildalton AG 11360 CT   Cottage: Bousd B 55835 CT   Tobermory B 00396 CN   Inveraray B 45917 CT   Iona A 45917 CT   Iona, cloister
B 77505 CN   Paisley, Coats Church A 43514 CN   Paisley drain B 56031 CN   Paisley drain, east B 56030 CN   Leuchars
B 08166 CN   Caerlaverock DF 3382 CN   Fort George A 28616 CN   Dunderave B8 CN   Glamis B 77501 CN   Kinnaird B 39101 CN   Falkland
Palace A 33073 CN   Kilchurn B 08153 CT   Sanquhar B 47664 CN   Falkland Town House B 39220 CN   Culross B 39165 CN   Glasgow, Park
Circus B 20163 CN   Glasgow, Egyptian Halls B 00521 CN   Inchinnan A 74204 CN   Edinburgh, Café Royal, James Watt tile ED 5239 CN
Edinburgh, Café Royal, sailing scene tile ED 5221 CN   Edinburgh, Café Royal, stained glass ED 5223 CN   Bonawe A 57323 CN   Newtongrange
ML 4040 CN   Tamdhu MO 1725 CN   Fraserburgh A 57235 CN   Glasgow, Conservatory B 31913 CN   Glasgow, School of Art A 37423 CT
Carrbridge B 55833 CT   Inveraray, Garron Bridge B 19136 CN   Forth Railway Bridge B 03280 CN

Front Cover   John Knox's House, Edinburgh
Back Cover   Former Co-operative building, 25-9 Causeyside Street, Paisley, Renfrew
District: detail of tile armorial in entrance vestibule
End Papers   Crathes Castle, Kincardine and Deeside: painted ceiling of the Muses'
Room *The National Trust for Scotland*

HMSO publications are available from:

HMSO Bookshops
71 Lothian Road, Edinburgh, EH3 9AZ
031-228 4181 Fax 031-229 2734
49 High Holborn, London, WC1V 6HB
071-873 0011 Fax 071-873 8200 (counter service only)
258 Broad Street, Birmingham, B1 2HE
021-643 3740 Fax 021-643 6510
Southey House, 33 Wine Street, Bristol, BS1 2BQ
0272 264306 Fax 0272 294515
9-21 Princess Street, Manchester, M60 8AS
061-834 7201 Fax 061-833 0634
16 Arthur Street, Belfast, BT1 4GD
0232 238451 Fax 0232 235401

HMSO Publications Centre
(Mail, fax and telephone orders only)
PO Box 276, London, SW8 5DT
Telephone orders 071-873 9090
General enquiries 071-873 0011
(queuing system in operation for both numbers)
Fax orders 071-873 8200

HMSO's Accredited Agents
(see Yellow Pages)
and through good booksellers